Healing Where You Are

*an Introduction
to Urban Foraging*

Suzannah Kolbeck

with illustrations by
Kim Mattison

akinoga press

Published by **akinoga press**.

Edited, designed, and typeset by mychael zulauf.

Cover art and illustrations by Kim Mattison.

This book is set in Bodoni 72.

ISNB-13: 979-8-9864742-0-5

For Lou Ann

Table of Contents

Introduction

Summer in the city: heat rising in waves from the sidewalk—unpleasantly humid—not a breath of wind, and no tree in the neighborhood to record it anyway. It is hard not to feel oppressed by the unrelenting Baltimore summer. Air slaps your face like a hot, damp washcloth; bones melt in the mid-day sun.

A plant sits squat and green, vibrant against cracked concrete. Its thin leaves and first hint of flowers shooting straight up from its center reveal this to be a plantain. She doesn't care that cigarette butts, plastic grocery bags, and charred spoons nestle in between her leaves. She persists, growing in the bit of soil between squares of sidewalk, in the shadow of a building collapsing in on itself.

On any given day, this plantain may be the only trace you'd encounter of the once sweeping and lush Piscataway land that Baltimore has cobbled itself together on. And each year, more and more of that land is engulfed by glass and steel and brick and concrete as the urban sprawl creeps on, often altering the local ecosystem in ways both unthinkable and devastating.

And yet, despite the sometimes-inflammatory relationship that exists between urban spaces and nature, nature endures.

Come closer. Look closer.

In even the most neglected of neighborhoods in your city, see what is growing in small spaces, poor soil, piles of rubble. There is green life here, hopeful plants with faces ever turned towards the sun:

Chickweed, a plant of love, amplification, and strength, with tiny flowers outlining the base of buildings, reaching out on tendrilled stalks lined with tiny hairs.

Plantain, available in every place, life medicine to indigenous people across North America, growing under the sign of Venus with abundant, healing, feminine energy.

Sweet-smelling pineappleweed, at its most potent and powerful when it emerges from desperate places, spreading its yellow-green cone-shaped buds low and energetically across a vacant lot.

These plants are thriving in neighborhoods in your city, undeterred by human neglect, pollution, and ignorance. With thoughtful attention, they ask us to pause, to take care. They invite us to mind what we are missing and to listen to the far-flung center of Self that gets lost in the daily navigation of these cramped urban environments.

This is a call to return to the wild spaces that persevere, within ourselves and in our urban places.

It is a call to explore your own urban space, to meet and know what lives there. To uncover respectfully and with gratitude the gifts that earth pushes forth and to forage them in a way that fosters a connection with, and a return to, your true nature.

Because even if we are, ourselves, native to a place, we are not truly of it until we learn its ecology. Knowing the plants outside your urban front door gives language and a sense of grounding more than any address. Paying attention to them allows you to locate yourself in a natural landscape and to become part of it: your block, your neighborhood, your city. Bioregionalism at the micro-level.

Come back to yourself. Look for the hopeful green things springing from the concrete that surrounds you. Consider this your invitation to urban foraging.

The nineteen plants highlighted in this book are common across North America; chances are good they are growing just outside your door, no matter where you live. Each entry comes with an illustration of the mature plant, basic information on her typical habitat, and some suggested preparations once she has been foraged.

Necessary but common-sense disclaimer: Always talk to your doctor or conduct your own research on each plant if you have concerns. None of the information in this book should be used to diagnose or treat a specific medical condition.

Getting Started

The Honorable Harvest

Urban foraging centers on the interaction between you and your environment. It's an act of reciprocity—plants arrive as you need them, and you gather them with respect and an eye toward sustainability. This cultivates a mindset of abundance and embodies what indigenous herbalist Robin Wall Kimmerer calls the Honorable Harvest. In her book, *Braiding Sweetgrass: Indigenous Wisdom, Scientific Knowledge and the Teachings of Plants,* she challenges us to develop a relationship with the natural world, instead of seeing it as simply a collection of resources for us to deplete.

To that end, consider implementing the following practices as you forage:

Never take the first plant you see. Consider your first sighting of a plant as a greeting, the shy welcome, an introduction to their home or habitat.

Ask permission before harvesting. When the second plant arrives before you, stop and ask permission before you harvest. This can take any form you like—a pause, a breath, an actual request. Anything that feels authentic to you.

Leave 2/3 of the plant behind. When it feels correct and appropriate, harvest no more than 1/3 of the plant in front of you (and in the proper manner). This practice often rewards you with a second and third harvest while leaving plenty for other creatures (and people) to enjoy. Note that some plants are considered invasive and can be harvested at will—but isn't it lovely to develop a relationship based on longevity and care?

Leave an offering. When I harvest any plant, my first offering is always a moment of gratitude and a deep, conscious breath for the blessing that I am experiencing. Sometimes I speak the gratitude out loud, but sometimes I am with a person who might find that odd—it's just as powerful inside my heart as it is spoken. I have also been known to leave a strand of hair, snipped with the same scissors with which I am foraging. I imagine a grateful bird, weaving it into her nest, or the soil that my hair has become a part of. Offer whatever feels like a gift from you – thought-full, genuine, and heartfelt.

Share. Finally, if you have an abundance, more than you need or can use, share it with people in your community. This generosity multiples the gift of the plant itself.

Where to begin

When you first commit to exploration and foraging, it can be tempting to amass a wide variety of plants to work with. You might be intent on building a home apothecary, and because herbal medicine takes time to craft, gathering plants in abundance when you see them seems like a good approach.

But consider this: it is more beneficial to really get to know the plants around you, even if it's just one or two, than to roam far afield in search of exotic or strange plants. It has been my experience that the remedies you need will often place themselves right in front of you if you are looking (and sometimes even when you're not). Those plants—the ones you constantly notice on your walk home, the ones that you are plucking out from between the steps of your front door, the so-called weeds that show up in your planters—they are often exactly what we need.

Develop a relationship with a few plants nearby. Notice when they are happiest—leaves and flowers shooting towards the sun or springing up after a summer shower—and take note of the changes in each plant as seasons change. Think of this careful attention as a tuning in—to yourself, to the natural world around you, to the abundance that is present in the everyday.

Nature wants you to see what she places in your path, and she will continue to put the same plant *in your way* in an effort to get you to stop and come closer.

Let's get this out of the way: there is nothing that you must have to begin foraging (with the notable exception of gloves for stinging nettle). Sure, you could drop a wad of cash on fancy bags and tools, but they are absolutely unnecessary. Foraging is available to everyone, with nothing in the way of possessions or consumerism required.

That said, as you forage, consider adding the following basic tools as you can:

• Gloves (the only real necessity for stinging nettle)
• A sturdy bag
• Plastic bags for plants (grocery bags work fine here)
• A spade or hori-hori (Japanese spade for digging roots)
• Scissors
• Notebook with a pen/pencil (you can use your phone for notes, but I like to make a sketch sometimes of plants)

A free plant ID app is also a good idea to confirm your identification. Two reliable options are PictureThis and iNaturalist. Which you choose is a matter of personal preference, but the basic version of both is free, and both are generally accurate.

In addition to the book you are holding, you might also eventually consider buying a guide to plants in your region (or checking one out of your local library). This helps to expand your knowledge over time but is not as valuable as walking out into your city and simply noticing what is around you.

As for processing your plants, don't trouble yourself with complicated dehydrators or fancy jars. You can begin to build your apothecary with glass jars and some kind of filtering device (e.g., clean t-shirt, coffee filter, or metal strainer). If you want to focus on drying plants, all you need is a piece of twine and a place to hang them to dry.

If you want to purchase something, a digital scale is very helpful when it comes to making medicine. Scales can be purchased at a big box store for ten bucks, or you can ask a neighbor if they have a scale to borrow. You can still make medicine without a scale, but your measurements will be more accurate (and your medicines more consistent).

Guidelines for safe foraging

An urban environment presents a variety of challenges when it comes to harvesting safe plants. Many cities have deeply contaminated soil, air, and water. In Baltimore, we routinely hear of raw sewage spilling by the millions of gallons into our waterways—the sewer system was designed, in fact, to overflow into the two major rivers running through the city and into the Inner Harbor of the Chesapeake Bay.

With that in mind, here are a few general guidelines:

- Avoid ditches with standing water
- Choose plants on the top or the middle of a hillside (not at the base of a hill)
- Look for visible contaminants (e.g., chemical containers, trash, spilled paint, etc.) and avoid gathering plants in that area
- Try to harvest at least 50 feet from a roadway and 25 feet from a path

It can seem challenging to find safe foraging spaces in your city—you might believe that the possibility of contaminants outweighs the medicinal possibilities, especially given the parameters above.

But consider a 2019 study from the East Bay area in Berkeley, California. Researchers looked at lead and cadmium levels found in soils, and then compared those levels to amounts found in washed greens. Tissue tests found that all levels of lead and heavy metals were below EPA standards, and chemical fertilizers and PCBs were not at detectable levels. What's more, these foraged foods often have a higher nutritional value than standard supermarket greens.

And it's worth noting that in the study above, samples of foraged wild foods were taken from industrial, commercial, and mixed-use high traffic urban areas in a part of the city that has a below average income level.

It's also an important understanding that many of the plants in this book function as a sort of clean-up crew for soil, leaving it better off than when their seeds first fluttered to the earth on a settled breeze and started to sprout. Respectful foraging honors the work of these plants and furthers the health of the places where we live.

What to Forage

Bee balm (Monarda fistulosa)

Bee balm—wild bergamot—friend of bees, butterflies, and other pollinating insects, symbolizes compassion and sympathy in its brilliant blooms and generous, expansive growth. Plants under Jupiter, as bee balm is, offer both a calming sweetness and a cleansing bitterness—a dependable comfort for our mutable, ever-changing bodies.

Bee balm is kin to mint and has the characteristic square and slightly fuzzy stem shared by this non-toxic plant family. She prefers sunny drought conditions and disturbed soil; find her swaying in the breeze on vacant lots and in elevated, open greenspaces. If soil is too wet, bee balm's rhizomatic roots rot and make her susceptible to powdery mildew. Even still, bee balm roots can survive vast disruption to bloom in unexpected places—the message of the plant's presence when she appears in our lives. She lifts light lavender, pink, or white tubular blooms to the sun beginning in July until summer's light wanes in early September. Know her also by crushing her sweetly bergamot or oregano-scented leaves. Harvest in the mornings after the dew has evaporated from her flowers and leaves.

As her name suggests, bee balm is a comfort to stings, scrapes, and bites, but she also offers internal benefits. Indigenous people in North America including the Winnebago, Blackfoot, and Ojibwe used bee balm to treat colds and congestion as well as digestive complaints including bloating, nausea, indigestion, and diarrhea. Bee balm contains thymol and carvetrol, antiseptic compounds found in mouthwash that treat gingivitis and other dental complaints. Finally, bee balm is a diffusive plant that warms and soothes nervous exhaustion, anxiety, and stress—a balm to the soul as well as the body.

Bee balm's flavor is reminiscent of a mild Earl Grey tea with undertones of oregano. In addition to the medicinal preparations below, bee balm makes a delicious jelly as well as a bright infused vinegar for salads and marinades.

Suggested preparation

Mouthwash: Place 2-3 tablespoons of flowers/leaves and 2 teaspoons of salt in a bowl. Cover with 1 cup boiling water and steep 20 minutes. Strain/chill and use 2x/day for canker sores or teeth issues.

Additionally:

- Use fresh or dried flowers in a tea for digestive upset
- Combine infused oil with beeswax to make a balm or a salve
- Place dried herbs and flowers in a sachet and add to the bath for a lung soothing steam

Bee balm (Monarda fistulosa)

Flowers are lavender,
pink, or white,
blooming in tubular
petals from the
center out.

Leaves are opposite, lanceolate
(lance-shaped), and hairless,
with shallow serrated edges.

Sturdy square stem supports
a plant that can grow
up to five feet tall.

Field Notes

Blue spruce tips (Picea pungens)

Associated with peace and protection, the spirit and medicine of blue spruce trees (and their tips) is gentle, attuned to the entire universe, and focused on healing. Nowhere is this more pronounced than in Old Tjikko, one of the world's oldest trees. This blue spruce sprang up from windborne seeds at the end of the Pleistocene, almost 10,000 years ago. While the current trunk of Old Tjikko is only a few hundred years old, as a clonal tree, she has survived by sprouting new roots when drooping branches contact the ground in order to strengthen old roots when the central trunk fades away. In this way, she has continued for years, and it is heartening to see the blue spruce trees on your block channel the quiet strength and stability of Old Tjikko.

Blue spruce trees gather and stand in a stereotypical conical shape on sunny stream banks and forest edges. In winter, their grey-green needles are short, stiff, and sharp enough to draw blood. Individual needles roll easily between gloved fingers (unlike yew, a poisonous lookalike, which sports flat needles that are striped white underneath). Aromatic grey-green bark circles the trunk in scales, and a grove of blue spruce will smell sweet. Although it can grow up to 75' tall with a branch spread of 20' in the wild, in urban spaces, the blue spruce is more restrained, only growing about as tall as an average human, and thus is fortunately accessible for medicine.

To harvest blue spruce tips, wait patiently for brown, papery cocoons that appear on the end of branches in the spring. Tips will emerge lime green, soft, and sticky with resinous medicine that smells of the forest and the sun, simultaneously. Harvesting from interior branches only—not the very top of the tree—allows for continued growth and health, for both tree and medicine maker.

Blue spruce tips are extraordinarily high in vitamin C, a traditional scurvy remedy for sailors across the globe, as well as potassium and magnesium. With shikimic acid, the same compound in Tamiflu, blue spruce tips are the medicine of choice for colds, coughs, and chest congestion, strengthening and protecting the immune system and acting as an expectorant to dissolve mucous. They also help to balance blood sugar and can be used externally to relieve muscle and joint aches.

Blue spruce tips offer a delicious refreshing burst of flavor. Very young tips can be eaten out of hand, puckeringly tart and mildly astringent in early spring, but they are not as tasty when they are longer than 2 inches. There are many culinary applications, both sweet and savory. Make spruce tips sugar and add to cookies (or salt for savory dishes). Spruce tips simple syrup can be used in cocktails and also in ice creams and sorbets. Pickle spruce tips for a burst of citrus flavor in salads. They can also be frozen if you won't be using them immediately.

Suggested preparation

Blue spruce herbal syrup: Add a tincture of blue spruce to an equal amount of simple syrup. To create simple syrup, combine sugar and water in a 1:1 ratio and heat until the sugar dissolves. Allow the syrup to cool, then combine with the blue spruce tincture.

If you would prefer to avoid alcohol in the preparation, add 1 cup of blue spruce tips to 1 quart of cool water and bring to a low boil. Simmer until the liquid is reduced by half, then remove from the heat and allow to steep with the lid on for at least 20 minutes (and up to several hours). Strain the blue spruce tips and add an equal amount of sugar to the pan (i.e., if you have a cup of liquid, add a cup of sugar). Heat until the sugar dissolves.

Additionally:

- Tincture spruce tips to ease coughs and lung congestion (with no sugar added)
- Create a spruce infused oil and make a balm or salve
- Use as a steam for quick relief of dry cough

Blue spruce (Picea pungens)

Short, sharp needles
require gloves for
safe harvest.

Papery brown wrappers
shed as buds grow.

Soft, light lime-green
buds emerge at the
end of each branch.

Field Notes

Blue vervain (Verbena hastata)

Blue vervain, also known as wild hyssop, native to North America's swamps, waste areas, and fields with poor soil, is a steady friend related to, but not actually in, the mint family. Her medicine reaches deeply into the autonomic nervous system to release muscles we did not know we were clenching—a gripping in the heart, knots in the belly, a tight pelvic floor. Blue vervain's bitterness allows us to gently, with steady hands, release our fears and move back into the world with softness and grace.

Look for blue vervain's four-sided stem that is grooved and sometimes purple-hued. She has no real scent but wafts a mushroom aroma when leaves are rubbed between fingers. Flowers with five purple or blue upright petals per flower climb long spikes arranged like candelabra June through September. Waiting for a full spike will leave you empty-handed—harvest by cutting just above leaf pairs when there are a reasonable number of flowers on the spike, and look for re-blooming later in the season. She is unmissable as she grows up to seven feet tall in the long, sluggish days of late summer.

Use blue vervain primarily as a tincture to calm the nervous system, to treat insomnia, and to soothe hormone-related migraines. She is a nervine, a tonic and a balm to anger and anxiety, cooling and relaxing a hot constitution. As with most plants with a bitter taste, blue vervain can also be used as a digestive aid. She is also helpful in bringing on delayed menstruation. She can be used topically to heal wounds—famously staunching Christ's stigmata—and also as an expectorant and diuretic. **A caution:** blue vervain is not good for people who are pregnant, and large doses can cause nausea and vomiting.

Blue vervain is most frequently used for a specific type of anxious person—the kind who has unwieldy high expectations of themselves and strains to meet them, no matter what. Vervain does not lessen the expectations but allows a person to let go of emotional tension held in the body because of them.

Suggested preparation

Tincture: Pack fresh vervain leaves and flowers into a pint (or ½-pint) jar. Cover with 80- or 100-proof vodka (all the way to the top) and allow it to sit for 10 to 12 weeks. Strain plant matter before use.

Additionally:

- Tea of blue vervain is usually bitter and best paired with a sweeter plant friend
- Make an infused oil for psoriasis, eczema, scrapes, and scratches

Blue vervain (Verbena hastata)

Purple or
blue flowers
appear from the
bottom to the top.

Fruits into nutlets
of four, single-
seeded sections.

Short lanceolate
leaves are opposite
in pairs, rough, and
serrated.

Field Notes

Burdock (Arctium lappa)

Burdock, in a subfamily of dandelion, is a healing, feminine plant under the sign of Venus. She nourishes and balances us with powers of protection and healing that rouse us from winter's last dregs into spring's lengthening days, guide us through late summer's balmy quiescence, and ease us into fall's withering light.

Burdock grows happily in poor soil and a variety of conditions. In her first year, burdock resembles others of her kind, with light green paired leaves in a low-growing basal rosette. These leaves are oblong or heart-shaped (cordate), grow on a single, purple-tinted leaf stalk, and can reach two feet by the end of the first year. To verify burdock in the first year, look for a leaf stalk that is furrowed, like celery. In her second year, burdock shoots towards the sky, reaching up to nine feet tall and sending forth globe-shaped purple flowers. These flowers begin to dry in the fall (becoming the eponymous bur), a sign that her second year is nearly through. Harvest roots in the fall of the first year or the spring of the second, and seeds as the flower becomes a bur.

The primary medicine of burdock is found in her roots (but her seeds are medicinal as well). Used often in a spring root tonic along with dandelion and yellow dock, the root of burdock is a nourishing blood tonic and stabilizer. Like ice melt in the spring surging through rivers and streams, burdock roots and seeds stimulate fluid movement in the body, clearing the lymph nodes, stimulating bile production (a standard function of bitter plants like burdock), and strengthening the liver. Burdock carries in her roots large amounts of inulin, a prebiotic that is helpful in weight loss, digestion, creating energy, and managing diabetes.

Externally, burdock is one of the most effective plant medicines for skin conditions. Her cooling, drying action works especially well on inflammatory skin conditions (e.g., acne and eczema). Burdock's effects are subtle and best experienced over time, but avoid her during pregnancy.

Burdock tastes strongly of the earth, the woods, and the meadow. She has a deeply soil-tasting root that is grounding, nourishing, and building. Burdock root (called gobo) is a part of daily Japanese cuisine as pickles, chips, and stir-fry.

Suggested preparation

Spring tonic tincture: Tincture burdock root by chopping cleaned burdock root coarsely and filling a pint jar 2/3 of the way. Cover the root with vodka and allow to steep for at least 10 weeks (but for best results 3-4 months).

When the tincture is ready, strain out the roots and combine the tincture with equal parts of dandelion and yellow dock tincture.

Additionally:

- Add a decoction to the bath for overall skin issues
- Use as a wash for inflammatory skin conditions
- Create a nourishing herbal infusion for the above internal benefits and to strengthen the immune system

Burdock* (Arctium lappa)

Wavy-edged leaves grow
up to four feet
long in the first
year!

Deeply-grooved stems
resemble celery

Hairy taproot has
dark brown skin
and an earthy fragrance.

* first-year growth

Burdock * (Arctium lappa)

Flowerheads are purple,
drying to a brown bur.

Grows up to
seven feet tall.

Leaves are oblong
or slightly cordate
(heart-shaped).

* second-year growth

Field Notes

Chickweed (Stellaria media)

Creeping low across thawing springs lawns, dripping over the edge of dormant winter planters, chickweed is one of the first greens of spring. She is a common yard weed with a cooling and drying aspect that supports us as we transition from winter to spring.

Chickweed is low-growing and sprawling, rarely reaching above seven inches at her tallest. Delicate, spindly stems are lined with soft hairs and well-spaced leaves that grow in opposite pairs alternating in direction as they travel up the stalk. The leaves themselves are oval with pointed tips. Delicate white flowers feature five deeply divided petals that lend chickweed her celestial moniker (*stellaria* comes from the Latin *stellar*, meaning star). A final test of identification: gently pull apart her stem. If there is no milky sap and the fibers in the stem stretch without breaking, you have found her. Harvest as much as you like—chickweed is abundant and resilient, another lesson from nature.

In spring, chickweed helps to move stagnation in the body. She is high in vitamin C and acts as mild diuretic and laxative. Because of these actions, she soothes urinary tract infections and relieves constipation. Chickweed works as an expectorant and emollient, relieving dry coughs and soothing lungs. She also works to purify the blood and lymphatic system and is anti-inflammatory, easing rheumatism, arthritis, cramps, and varicose veins. Try chickweed externally for a variety of conditions including acne, eczema, psoriasis, rashes, minor burns, insect bites, and scrapes.

Chickweed has a mild flavor similar to corn silk and can be eaten raw in salads and on sandwiches. Use her anywhere you might use sprouts.

Suggested preparation

Nourishing herbal infusion: Place 2 ounces of chickweed in a quart jar and cover with boiling water. Allow to cool steep at room temperature, then place in the fridge for 24 hours. Strain plant material and drink a cup or two a day as needed.

Additionally:

- Create an infused oil or balm/salve for targeted relief from skin irritations
- Take internally as a tincture (for conditions above, but also for hot flashes when taken daily)
- Simmer fresh chickweed in a 1:1 ratio of vinegar to water and cool before applying as a poultice

Chickweed (Stellaria media)

Oval leaves grow
in opposite pairs.

Flowers have five
deeply divided
petals and resemble
stars.

Spindly, low-growing
and spreading plant.

Field Notes

Chicory (Chichorium intybus)

Chicory, symbol of frugality, faithfulness in love, and bitter longing. She is the sacred daughter of Jupiter and holds a place in Linnaeus's floral clock in Uppsala, Sweden at 5 a.m. and 11 a.m. (the hours of her blooms' opening and closing). Chicory also answers to the name of succory or turnsole.

Chicory loves disturbed areas that include fields, roadsides, and highway medians. She grows up to two feet tall (and reaches down with a similarly deep taproot) on a medium green skinny, hairy stalk. Flowers that open only in sunny weather (and close up tight on cloudy days) appear in stalkless blue rays fixed tight to the stem and are no more than 1 ½" across. Chicory grows in a bunched group with stems that feature spreading, scraggly lateral branches with leaves resembling a dandelion's at the base before getting smaller as they crawl up the stem. She loves compact soil and sends her roots deep to break it up and to access vital minerals in the earth. Confirm her identification by the milky sap that oozes from a cut stem. She has no toxic lookalikes, which makes her an excellent plant for those new to foraging. Gather chicory flowers in the moonlight when they bloom, and harvest roots in the fall.

Chicory also has similar properties to dandelion and is high in vitamins (A, B, C, K, and P) as well as potassium, calcium, and sodium. She is a balancing, blood building, alterative plant that stimulates the flow of bile while maintaining a slightly sedative effect. She also contains lactones—these work on the opioid receptors in the brain to impart a feeling of well-being that is good for easing anxiety. Chicory's bitter properties stimulate the appetite and improve digestion. Naturally-occurring terpenes and other substances in chicory have been found effective in treating jaundice, malaria, gall and kidney stones, and ulcers. Her roots are used to treat fever and headache and to lower blood pressure. They also contain large amounts of inulin (a type of fiber), which can be made into a safe and gentle laxative. Externally, the milky sap in the stem can be applied to warts to dry them up and to treat acne. Chicory should be avoided if pregnant.

Chicory root is famously bitter, a quality that has historically been capitalized on as a coffee extender. She is known to counteract the effects of too much caffeine, which might explain why the coffeepot is always on in the south, where coffee with chicory remains a staple.

Suggested preparation

Anxiety relief tincture: Make a tincture using the entire plant for a powerful ally against anxiety. Pack chopped roots, leaves, and flowers into a pint jar and cover with 80- or 100-proof vodka. Allow it to steep for at least 10 weeks, then strain the plant matter.

Additionally:

- Create a decoction of roots for a face wash
- Chicory tea with flowers is best for digestive issues
- Make the root into a syrup (or dry it in the oven and grind for coffee or tea)

Chicory (Chichorium intybus)

Scraggly, branching
plant that grows
in sparse clusters.

Flower petals are
square-tipped and
fringed in stalkless
rays.

Leaves resemble a dandelion's
at the base of the plant.

Field Notes

Cleavers (Galium aparine)

Cleavers, spring's sweet tonic, also known as bedstraw or goosegrass (two other medicinal plants in the family Galium). Indigenous people, watching deer lay their fawns on beds of cleavers to rest, called her *deer medicine*—a cooling, drying, supportive daughter of the Moon related to artists and beauty.

Cleavers is a creeping perennial found in cultivated land, twining through hedges and woven throughout thick scrub. She is light to dark green, spindly, and tall, with stems that can reach nearly six feet. The entire plant is covered with tiny, sticky hairs—they cling to you as you brush past. Look for a tall, graceful plant with thin leaves that are stalkless and radiating in groups of six or eight around one node (point) on the stem. Tiny flowers rise in clusters from the axils of the stalk (where leaf and stalk connect). Look to harvest during a brief two-week period from late spring to early summer before she gets stringy and spread out. After, her medicine will be less powerful and her stem will become woody and tough. To ensure you have G. aparine, crush the plant and smell—a light vanilla scent means bedstraw.

Cleavers's medicine is a tonic that is nourishing (and safe for young children), used to gradually restore health and vitality to sluggish winter bodies over time. She promotes movement of fluid through the body—including the lymphatic system, the bladder, and the kidneys—and is high in vitamin C. Her most powerful internal use is as a nourishing herbal infusion. In this form, she treats people who have nervousness, sympathetic excess, a feeling of fussiness, insatiability, irritability, and a general feeling of being not oneself. Externally, she is a soothing wash for eczema or for skin tickles and itches.

Avoid cleavers if you are pregnant or nursing. Those with high blood pressure or on blood thinning medications should also steer clear of cleavers. If brushing up against cleavers causes a skin irritation, do not use in any preparation.

Culinarily, cleavers seeds are one of a few botanicals that can be used as a coffee substitute. As with coffee, the taste is slightly bitter and astringent. She loses much of her medicinal properties upon drying, so use cleavers fresh for best results.

Suggested preparation

Nourishing herbal infusion: The best spring medicine for cleavers brings for balance and harmony in the body in a nourishing herbal infusion. Cover 2 ounces of plant matter with boiling water in a quart jar and allow to steep for 24 hours, first at room temperature until it cools and then in the 'fridge. Strain out plant matter and drink one or two cups daily.

Additionally:

- Preserve as a tincture or in a vinegar or oxymel
- Externally, create a wash with water for skin ailments

Cleavers (Galium aparine)

Hooked prickles
line every
leaf and stem.

Tiny white flowers
emerge from leaf axils.

Slender leaves
group in whorls
of up to eight.

Field Notes

Dandelion (Taraxacum officianale)

Dent de lion, the flower of the toothy lion, the dandelion is a universe in a single plant: sun in its multi-petaled flower; moon in its fluffy, seedy puffball; stars in the seeds that float for up to five miles, released by the breeze or a hopeful, wish-filled breath.

Dandelion is in the family sunflower, arriving in bright yellow as early as February and as late as June (with a second flowering in August). Look for dandelion in fragile, damaged soil; cracks in the sidewalk; open spaces—anywhere there is enough dirt for a seed to rest. She grows toothed leaves in a ground-hugging basal rosette, and sunlight affects her leaf characteristics. Dandelions basking in fields with full sun have deeply-toothed, thick green leaves, while her shady sisters' leaves are pale, thin, and only slightly serrated. Rain on the way locks a mature puffball up tight, and this *shepherd's clock* marks morning and evening with flowers that open and close with sun's rise and set.

Harvest leaves first on a dry spring day, followed by flowers once morning's dew has evaporated. Roots are harvested depending on their use. For a bitter digestive tonic, harvest spring roots; those with Type 2 diabetes will use the sweeter roots of late fall to capture ample inulin after dandelion's last flowering.

Under Jupiter, a planet of great good fortune and beneficence, dandelion breaks up imbalances in the body when used long-term. A great benefit to liver function, dandelion is high in potassium, magnesium, iron, and vitamins A and C. Her roots contain between 25 and 40% inulin, best accessed in a decoction to help the body create energy and better use dandelion's nutrients. Dandelion is a diuretic and a gentle laxative. Apply dandelion's fresh milky sap to remove warts and corns.

Young, tender dandelion leaves are a delicious way to welcome spring. Infuse vinegar with fresh leaves, too, or create an oxymel to make salad dressings and flavor soups and sauces (or just take by the tart-sweet spoonful to harness her sunny power).

Suggested preparation

Root decoction: Chop 2 ounces of spring roots and cover them in 2 cups of water in a saucepan. Bring to a low simmer and hold there until the water is reduced by half. Cool and use within a week in spring for energy, digestion, and detoxing (use fall roots to make a digestive decoction).

Additionally:

- Tincture fresh root for anti-inflammatory and cooling benefits
- Drink dandelion tea of fresh leaves as a gentle diuretic and laxative
- Rub dandelion flower infused oil into joints and muscles to ease inflammation

Dandelion (Taraxacum officinale)

Each soft, bristly pappus carries a single seed.

Leaf margins are toothed but hairless

Long, tapering taproot provides minerals to the plant and the soil around it.

Field Notes

Elderberry (Sambucas nigra)

Of all medicinal plants to be foraged in cities, elderberry is arguably one of the most recognizable. Long known as *the medicine of the country people*, this powerful plant symbolizes purification, love, compassion, and zealousness. The ancient Celts believed that a spirit who mustn't be angered lived in elderberry, and that the plant itself was a door between the realms. Elderberry is medicine under the sign of Venus and is often planted for protection.

Elderberry is in the honeysuckle family and appears in a variety of shades depending on the species. She is a tree-like shrub that sends short roots into poor soil in either sun or partial shade, eventually reaching heights (and sometimes widths) of up to 19 feet. Elderberry's short trunk sends out twiggy branches with a green spongy pith inside. She is deciduous—look for dark green- or purple-tinted pinnate leaves situated in pairs opposite each other on twigs. She flowers from June to July in umbels—the wind-blown-umbrella shape. These flowers give way to drooping clusters of dark purple (nearly black) fruits in late summer. Use caution and prudence when harvesting flowers for spring medicine—if you harvest all flowers, no berries will appear.

Elderberry is well-known and widely used for allergies, respiratory health, rheumatism, viral infections (including herpes and shingles), and flu. She is anti-viral and anti-inflammatory, with decongestant, fever-breaking, and cooling actions in the body. Her berries are loaded with flavonoids, beta carotene, iron, potassium, and vitamins A and C. Elderberry is also used externally for burns and wounds, but her main strength lies inside the body. Only the berries and flowers are used as medicine, and the berries must be cooked or dried.

Elderberries have an earthy, tart flavor that blends well with other berries in culinary uses. The taste of the flower is more subtle, with hints of pear scent that influences the perception of the taste.

Suggested preparation

Elderberry syrup: Place elderberries in a saucepan and add water just to cover. Heat to soften the berries, then strain through a sieve or cheesecloth to extract the juice (discard berry pulp). Add sugar/honey, stir to dissolve, and allow to cool before decanting to a jar in the 'fridge.

A note: adding dried flowers to this syrup makes creates a febrifuge and a diaphoretic – a sweat-inducing, fever-breaking treatment.

Additionally:
- Make a healing tincture with flowers
- Combine an infused oil of dried flowers and dried berries with beeswax to make an anti-inflammatory salve or balm
- Create a flu-treating tea by combining equal parts fresh elderflower, fresh yarrow flower and leaf, and fresh mint with boiling water, steeping for 45 minutes and sipping throughout the day

Elderberry (Sambucus nigra)

Creamy white,
five-petaled
flowers cluster
in umbels.

Leaflets are
lightly-toothed
and appear in
opposite
pairs.

Look for deep purple
berries on drooping
red stems where
flowers were.

Field Notes

Goldenrod (Solidago)

With her sunny, brilliant inflorescence of blooms, goldenrod is an insect-pollinated medicinal plant who is often falsely blamed for flaring seasonal allergies. She is soothing and healing, just like the warm rays of the sun that rule her astrologically.

Goldenrod is found anywhere there is abundant sunshine: in fields, meadows, open woods, and along trails. There are over 130 different species of goldenrod, all of which can be used for medicine and many of which can be found in urban areas on vacant lots and in wild greenspaces. She grows anywhere from one to eight feet tall on thick stems with tiny (painless) spikes that are barely visible. Her leaves are alternate, thin, slender, mostly smooth-edged, usually less than three inches long, and tend to not extend past the leaves at the base of the plant. The main stem grows vertical until flowers are imminent, which prompts the growth of multiple horizontal branches covered in tiny green buds that burst into bright yellow to deep gold individual disc and ray flowers. It is common for flowers to grow in clusters of 30 or so, some appearing to line a branch, others forming cones. Flowers appear late summer to early fall, and an early flowering generally predicts a harsh winter.

Finalize her identification by crushing the leaves or tasting flowers. Most goldenrod smell faintly of salt or resin, and sweet goldenrod (Solidago odora) tastes like licorice. Proper identification is crucial, as goldenrod does have toxic lookalikes that include plants in the aster family (e.g., ragwort and groundwort). These plants will often release a cloud of pollen when shook – goldenrod does not. Goldenrod's flowers contain her medicine. Harvest by cutting just above the branching stem to encourage lush re-growth.

Goldenrod is used for medicine and dye (a rich, luxurious yellow). She is good for allergies (including hay fever and cat dander) as well as upper respiratory infections. One of her main uses is for urinary tract issues, including infections, blockages, kidney stones, and inflammation. Goldenrod is anti-inflammatory and antiseptic and can also be used topically to ease sore muscles and heal wounds (hence the English common name *wound wort*).

The Latin *solidago* translates loosely into *making whole*. Goldenrod gently relieves the mild melancholy that can occur as daylight wanes. Celebrate the harvest and restful time to come with wild-fermented goldenrod soda or a pan of goldenrod cornbread.

Suggested preparation

Tea: Use two tablespoons of fresh goldenrod flowers and leaves or one tablespoon of dried per cup of hot water. Pour boiling water over the goldenrod and allow to steep for 15 minutes before straining and drinking. Sweeten with honey if desired, or add a little mint if you prefer.

Additionally:

- Make an infused oil from dried flowers (and turn into salve or a balm if you prefer) for healing massage
- Create a supportive tincture for fall allergy season
- Use in an oxymel for sweet/tart support in the winter time
- Drink as a nourishing herbal infusion to relieve UTIs and for upper respiratory infections and to ease into winter

Goldenrod (Solidago)

Inflorescence includes three dozen disc and ray florets on each single stem.

Goldenrod stems do not branch until they flower.

Narrow, almost grass-like leaves are smooth, with a distinct scent for each species.

Field Notes

Lemon balm (Melissa officinalis)

Lemon balm, also known as sweet Melissa after her Latin name, is a highly fragrant plant of love, success, and healing. Ruled by Venus, lemon balm is also a child of the moon and is associated with water—a calming, relaxing plant friend who is a gentle healer.

Growing no higher than three feet (and often just as wide), lemon balm is a bushy perennial that is at home in poor soil found along roadsides and in fields. Lemon balm is in the mint family and has mint's characteristic square stem. Her leaves are lightly serrated, oval-trending cordate (heart-shaped) and smell distinctly of citrus when crushed. Lemon balm flowers are tiny and two-lipped, ranging in color from white to a very faint pink and appearing in most areas from June to September. To harvest large amounts for medicine, wait until flower buds or flowers appear, as this is the time when volatile oils are most concentrated. Use scissors to cut just above a leaf pair, leaving at least 1/3 of the plant and at least six inches of stem to encourage new growth.

Lemon balm is beneficial medicine that strengthens your heart and your spirit. She is a powerful nervine, calming anxiety and improving focus (safe for children with ADHD). Her carminative action relieves constipation and helps with digestion. She also eases inflammation both internally and externally. Use her to treat insect bites, wounds, cold sores, shingles, and eczema. Avoid her if you have hypothyroidism as she can affect thyroid function.

Lemon balm is delicious in many culinary applications. Her fresh leaves can be used anywhere you might use lemon zest—even in cookies and cakes.

Suggested preparation

Tincture: Create an easy, stress-relieving lemon balm tincture by adding chopped fresh pant material (leaves, stems, and flowers) to a pint jar and covering with 80- or 100-proof vodka. Steep for at least ten weeks, then strain plant material. Mix in fresh mint leaves for a refreshing touch and to ease the digestive upset that sometimes comes with anxiety.

Additionally:

- Drink daily as a nourishing herbal infusion
- Relax with a tea of fresh or dried leaves for digestion
- Create a wash for widespread rashes
- Use infused oil in a balm or a salve to treat inflammatory skin conditions

Lemon balm (Melissa officianalis)

Lightly - toothed
leaves grow in
opposite pairs.

Look for flowers in the leaf
axil - where the upper part
of the leaf meets stem.

Upright, branching, square
stem is covered in
microscopic hairs.

Field Notes

Mugwort (Artemisia vulgaris)

Named for the Greek goddess, Artemesia vulgaris is often most recognized by her common name – mugwort. This simple name hints at her previous life spent flavoring beer in Europe (hence the mug in the name), but that's not all this visionary plant of Venus and the moon can do. She is known as *the mother of all herbs*, a universal herb for protection and prophecy used throughout the world.

Mugwort loves abundant sunshine, especially in disturbed areas filled with other weeds. She starts out thin and willowy in the spring but finishes strong and lush by the end of summer, with bushy stems that spread with rhizomes and can reach up to six feet tall. A tell-tale identifier is hidden under mugwort's leaves. Flip one over and compare—the top of the leaf will be light to dark green and smooth, while the underside is a distinctive fuzzy silver or silvery-green. Her leaves resemble a chrysanthemum's and also have a slight odor when crushed. Leaves alternate on a furrowed stem, becoming smaller and more narrow as they climb and growing up to three inches across and four inches wide.

Mugwort is powerful plant medicine. Her bitter properties improve digestion and support liver function. Mugwort is also soothing to the nervous system and mildly sedating. She helps regulate uneven menstrual cycles and relieves joint pain. Mugwort can be used as a vermifuge to expel intestinal parasites (for this action she has been called *wormwood* or *felon herb*). Externally, mugwort calms raised, itchy scars and can remove warts when applied as a poultice of fresh leaves. When smoked (or used as a powder in moxibustion), mugwort produces vivid dreams and enhances a dreamer's recall of them. Even placing a stem underneath your pillow at night produces these effects.

Mugwort's effects are so powerful that people who are pregnant should avoid her in any form—even to touch her leaves. The same emmenagogic and cholagogic/choleretic properties that work as a laxative and increase bile production can induce uterine bleeding and even miscarriage.

Mugwort is a magical plant that connects us with the divine feminine. She helps us to let go, to contact our wild inner life through dreams and visions. Do not use mugwort in any preparation for longer than a week at a time.

Suggested preparation

Mugwort herbal smoke: Combine 2 tablespoons of dried mullein, 1 tablespoon dried mugwort, ½ teaspoon dried lemon balm, 1 teaspoon of water, and 1 drop of honey. Mix well and use your favorite smoking apparatus. This is an especially powerful blend for dreaming and relaxation.

BIG WARNING: Do not smoke mugwort anywhere that people who are pregnant will gather. And if you are not already a smoker, skip this preparation.

Additionally:

- Tincture fresh mugwort to support the liver and treat parasites
- Sip as tea with one tablespoon dried leaves per cup of boiling water (no more than two cups per day) to enhance digestion
- Use as a soothing wash on itchy scars
- Pack a protective sachet of dried leaves for travel
- Create a dream pillow with fresh herbs for lucid or prophetic dreams

Mugwort (Artemisia vulgaris)

Deeply cut and lobed
leaves of dark green
get smaller at the
top of the plant.

Underside of leaves is
dramatically different
from the top - a light
silvery green.

Stems are deeply furrowed
at the base, becoming
purple-hued and woody
as they age.

Field Notes

Mullein (Verbascum thapsus)

Magical, mythical mullein—plant medicine for courage and health, love and protection. She is ruled by the moon and offers powerful support for fertility and a passion for prediction. In the tradition of the Ozarks, point a flower stalk of mullein at your beloved's house. If the stalk rises, your love is returned.

But mullein is more than divination. Like her unrelated friend the dandelion, mullein is committed to improving her surroundings. She thrives in the poor soil of wastelands, ditches, rocky hillsides, and abandoned areas, healing the earth as she grows. Mullein's deep taproot has fibrous branching roots that break up compacted soils. Once soil health is repaired, mullein dies off and moves to the next area that needs attention. She grows in a two-year cycle. In the first year, recognize mullein's low-growing basal rosette of wooly silvery-green ovate leaves. These leaves emerge small and tender in the spring but eventually grow as long as a foot and as wide as five inches each. Leaves alternate in a whorl to funnel water to the roots of the plant.

In mullein's second year, she sends a single flower stalk skyward and can reach heights of up to ten feet. The flower stalk is densely clustered with yellow five-petaled flowers. Blooms arrive throughout the summer from the bottom of the stalk to the top, with flowers opening before sunrise and closing by mid-afternoon. Harvest leaves from the middle of the plant in springtime before the flower stalk appears. Roots can be harvested by digging or pulling up the whole plant, and flowers can be plucked from the stalk as needed. Note that mullein seeds are toxic and should not be consumed.

Mullein has incredible healing properties for the lungs. She contains saponins to help loosen mucous in the lungs, easing dry cough and making it more productive. Because mullein heals damage to the lungs, her most frequent use is for any respiratory complaint (including pneumonia and tuberculosis), but she can also be smoked as a tobacco substitute as an aid to stop smoking. Her mildly sedating properties help ease irritation that comes with quitting tobacco smoking, too.

Mullein is anti-inflammatory and anti-viral – this makes her an excellent ally for treating colds, UTIs, viruses, and gastrointestinal issues due to inflammation. Her cooling, moistening properties soothe the body both internally and externally; use mullein topically for bruises, tumors, rheumatic pain, hemorrhoids, and lower back pain, too. She treats earaches (safe enough for children) and eases migraines, too.

Regardless of how you use her, strain all preparations carefully, as mullein's tiny hairs can be irritating. For drying, remove the tough midrib with a sharp knife before curing or hanging to dry.

Suggested preparation

Respiratory tincture blend: Tincture mullein on its own for healthy, clear lungs, or make a tincture blend with marshmallow (Althaea officinalis). Make separate tincture of each plant (chop fresh plant matter and cover with vodka, steep for ten weeks, then strain), or create a blend by combining a 1:1 ratio by weight of mullein and marshmallow before covering with vodka, steeping, and straining as usual.

Additionally:

- Dried leaves make a healing herbal smoke (try equal parts mullein, mint, and thyme for respiratory healing)
- Infuse oil with flowers and leaves for earaches and as a chest rub for bronchial congestion

Mullein* (Verbascum thapsus)

Tiny hairs called
trichomes give
mullein its
velvety feel.

Long, grey-green
oval leaves
emerge and unfold
in a basal rosette.

The center leaves
have smooth margins
that begin to ripple
as they grow.

* first-year growth

Mullein * (Verbascum thapsus)

Densely clustered yellow-
petaled, stalkless flowers
give way to seed in
autumn.

Wooly silver leaves
cover a single stem
that can reach
up to eight feet.

Deep, branching roots
break up and improve soil.

* second-year growth

Field Notes

Pineappleweed (Matricaria discoidea)

For energy and ease, pineappleweed is plant medicine that works on both ends of the spectrum. This modest member of the Asteraceae family (think sunflowers and daisies) is native to northwest North America and Asia, but has slowly spreading across the globe. She is found under the astrological protection of the sun and is used by the Cheyenne in their sun dance ceremony.

Pineappleweed carries a lesson for us all in that her best medicine comes from the most stressed of her plants. To that end, look for her in very poor soil and sunny open spaces like lawns, parks, and roadsides. She is delicate and unobtrusive—her finely dissected, feathery leaves are no more than two inches long, less than an inch wide, and topped with tiny rayless flowers. Pineappleweed's flower buds resemble upside-down greenish yellow strawberries with tiny white half-moon flower petals snugged up against the base of the bud. The whole plant is easily missed, being low-growing and spreading. She has no toxic lookalikes, but the final test is scent—crush her flowers and inhale her sweet, distinctive pineapple scent. Harvest individual flowers when they are more yellow than green, or cut entire stems to use the leaves as well.

Pineappleweed is related to German chamomile and has many of the same benefits. She relieves anxiety and is good for menstrual cramps, pain, and nausea. Her flowers are a nervine that calms as they prevent bloating, stomach cramps, and constipation. Pineappleweed is an anti-inflammatory that can treat parasitic infection to improve nutrient uptake. She also soothes itchy rashes and sores and eases inflammatory skin conditions (e.g. acne and eczema). People allergic to the family Asteraceae should avoid pineappleweed, as should people who are pregnant.

The simplest way to consume pineappleweed for her energy-giving properties is to chew a few fresh flowers—this will provide a quick burst of hopeful and uplifting energy.

Suggested preparation

Pineappleweed tea: Sip a relaxing tea with two tablespoons of dried pineappleweed flowers per each cup of hot water. Steep for ten minutes and serve with honey, if desired.

Additionally:

- Use as a digestive tincture of fresh flowers
- Prepare a nourishing herbal infusion with dried leaves and flowers for relief of gas and as a laxative
- Create a wash using a vinegar infusion of fresh flowers for skin inflammation

Pineappleweed (*Matricaria discoidea*)

Fully grown flowerheads are less than ⅛" in diameter.

Flat white petals cling to a central bud.

Feathery leaves on a low-growing, spreading plant.

Field Notes

Plantain (Plantago major)

"Take thee some new infection to the eye/And the rank poison of old will die." So counsels Benvolio to a heartbroken Romeo, not yet in love with Juliet but pining for Rosalind still. Romeo responds that plantain leaf is a good remedy for a "broken shin," a minor pain compared to a broken heart. Plantain—the elastic bandage of Romeo's time—may not have healed the scars of love, but she offers powerful medicine for many other of life's slings and arrows. She marked the passage of the white man settling the west in North America, earning her the nickname *white man's tears*, but even this trail of woe does not diminish the benefits of this plant. Some of the same indigenous people translated her name as *life medicine*, reflecting plantain's importance in their culture.

For beginning urban foragers, plantain is a safe and easy path to medicine. She has no toxic lookalikes and grows abundantly in poor soil, including that found in sidewalk cracks and at the base of buildings. Leaves are low-growing and can be ovate (Plantago major) or lance-shaped and thin (Plantago lanceolate). Both grow in a rosette shape—to verify your ID, gently break the leaf stem to see if veins remain attached. This loving plant (under Venus) sends a thin stalk of densely clustered flowers into the air in early spring and autumn, flowers that imperceptibly give way to seeds. Harvest as much as you like at any point in her life cycle—she will come back, and stronger.

Plantain is a good source of iron and vitamins A and C, and she contains two vital ingredients to help heal inflammation, rashes, cuts, itching, and bug bites: allantoin, a cell proliferant that speeds healing, and acubin, an anti-toxin that fights infection. As a poultice, plantain works to draw out wound impurities, cooling and soothing injuries. Children at play can harvest her leaves, chew them up and apply directly to ease a bee sting. Most applications of plantain occur topically, but she has internal uses as well. She treats heartburn, indigestion, and diarrhea. She is also a supportive treatment for ulcers and IBD and encourages a productive cough.

Plantain is a topical wonder, a friend to anyone caught in the woods by a bee, a sting, or a scrape. Chew fresh plant matter and create a poultice for itches and wounds—the taste is mildly of asparagus. This flavor can be enhanced in the sauté pan, too.

Suggested preparations

Infused oil: The most common preparation for plantain is infused oil. This is also the first step to making a balm or a salve. The basic ratio for infused oil is one part dried plant matter to five parts oil. So if you use one ounce of plant matter, top with five ounces of infusing oil. Another method is to simply pack half a pint jar with dried plant matter and then cover with the oil of your choice. Make sure that the plant matter is completely covered. Allow this to steep for three or more months. You can speed the process by warming it slightly and then keeping it in a warmer room. Do not place this in the sun, as it will diminish the plant's medicine.

Additionally:

- Sip a nourishing herbal infusion or tea (a less common use)
- Use as a tincture for quick relief of cough

Plantain (Plantago major)

Midsummer, densely clustered
flowers on a stalk give
way to seeds by autumn.

Underside of
leaves may be
tinted purple

Leaves are broad and ovate
with parallel raised veins
running the length of the leaf

Field Notes

Red Clover (Trifolium pratense)

Plants found under Mercury are noted for the ability to bring balance, to calm an anxious mind, and to corral a body's racing energy. Red clover is one such Mercurial plant, with both systemic benefits and acute symptom relief.

From May to September, red clover roots herself in fields, roadsides, and abandoned lots and yards. She stands either erect on stems of up to two feet tall or sprawls across the ground, never gaining more than ½" of height. Recognize red clovers by her leaves and flowers. Her leaves are smooth-edged and appear in threes (hence the symbolism of the common name, trefoil) that are dark green and patterned with a lighter green chevron on each. Flowers are sessile, emerging directly from a slender stem with no individual stalk. Pink or deeply red flowers (but not white—a different kind of clover) are tubular and spread outward in opposite directions. Bees and people alike love red clover's honey-like scent. Harvest her sweet-smelling blossoms one or two weeks after she begins to bloom, early in the morning when she is still bathed in dew (so as to preserve her rosy hue).

The best (and most common) use of red clover is in support of people born with female reproductive organs. Red clover contains phytoestrogens that bind to endogenous estrogen receptors. These receptors help to regulate female reproductive health in all phases of life. She eases symptoms of menopause, including hot flashes and vaginal dryness, but also supports fertility, soothes menstrual cramps, and relaxes the body/mind with mildly sedative properties. She is also used to treat systemic irritation, including gout, arthritis, asthma, and inflammatory skin disorders. She is a sweet alterative, a cooling and expectorant plant who helps to relieve stagnation and combat high cholesterol. But as kind as red clover is to female reproductive systems, avoid her during pregnancy. Additionally, red clover has blood thinning properties and should not be used while on prescription blood thinners or before surgeries.

Red clover is heavy with symbolism. Dreaming about her means good things are coming your way, and finding her four-leafed variation predicts love, luck, success, and protection.

Suggested preparation

Supportive tincture: Use fresh flowers to create a tincture that relieves systemic inflammation in the body. People with female reproductive organs may also find relief from the symptoms of menopause and peri-menopause when they combine a red clover tincture with a raspberry leaf tincture. These can be made separately and mixed or created as a single tincture in a 1:1 ratio.

Additionally:

- Use as a nourishing herbal infusion
- Blend into an herbal syrup to relieve cough and indigestion
- Use as an herbal smoke (alone or in a blend) to clear the lungs and treat asthma and dry cough
- Create a soothing wash for skin inflammation

Red clover (Trifolium pratense)

Flower color ranges from
whisper-pink to
rich magenta.

Bold chevrons
distinguish red
clover from white.

Oval-ovate or slightly
obovate leaflets appear
in groups of three.

Field Notes

Stinging Nettle (Urtica diotica)

Stinging nettle is one of Spring's first offerings, nourishing and stabilizing winter bodies that crave sharp tastes. Step lightly in rusted areas where metal has gone to dissolve slowly back into the earth—stinging nettle is at home in such places.

Look first for heart-shaped, light green leaves that turn darker and more pointed with age. Stinging nettle has a sharp bite that earns her name—tiny crystal trichomes, hairs filled with formic acid and histamines line each stem and petiole and leaf, toothed leaf edges a warning of her sting. Wear gloves to harvest before flowers appear—tiny white, green, or yellow densely clustered whorls drop from the connection between leaf and stem.

She grows in clusters, spreading with rhizomatic roots that creep and branch along with windborne seeds, sent aloft by summer breezes. Look for new growth again in early autumn, and take all you please—stinging nettle is generous and prolific wherever you find her, a way to ground yourself and connect deeply to the earth during transitional times.

Stinging nettle is one of the most nutritious plants you can forage, with iron, more protein than beans, and more magnesium and calcium than spinach.
A daughter of Mars (which explains her prickly nature), stinging nettle reduces inflammation and works as a tonic for kidneys. She is good for allergies, asthma, anemia, chronic weakness, high blood pressure, and skin diseases. She filters uric acid to treat gout and increases milk production for lactating people. Dried nettle seeds are considered an adaptogen that supports adrenal and endocrine health.
Use cautiously if you are taking sedatives, lithium, or blood pressure medication.

Nettle has a funky taste that is a little bit grass, a little bit earth, and a little bit musty. She is a nutrient-packed substitute for any dish that uses spinach, with the highest amount of protein in any foraged plant. Nettle pesto is especially delicious and nutritionally supportive. Nettle seeds can be taken medicinally, or they can be used like any other kind of seed – sprinkled on salads, baked into crackers and bread, or sprinkled on top of morning yogurt.

Suggested preparation

Stinging nettle tea: Place 1 tablespoon of dried nettle leaves in a heatproof cup and cover with boiling water. Allow to steep for ten minutes while you muddle one slice of fresh lemon with 1 tablespoon of honey in a pint glass. Top the lemon and honey with ice, then add the steeped nettle tea. Add a splash of sparkling water and some fresh mint.

Additionally:

- Dry fresh nettle and make a nourishing herbal infusion for kidney support
- Create a tincture of leaves for quick allergy relief, or tincture dried seeds for a boost in mood, energy, and libido
- Use infused nettle oil to make a balm or salve

Stinging nettle (Urtica diotica)

Serrated margins
on leaves that
are 2-4" long.

Small, stinging hairs line
stems, petioles, and the
underside of
leaves

Cordate (heart-shaped)
leaves grow opposite
each other.

Field Notes

Yarrow (Achillea millefolium)

Achilles millefolium, named after the war hero Achilles who used her thousand leaves to treat battle wounds, is a strong ally cloaked in a fine, delicate appearance. A loving plant found under Venus, yarrow contains potent healing medicine. She is a beautifully flowered perennial, friend to pollinator and people alike.

Yarrow is often planted in ornamental gardens for her feathery-leaved appearance and clusters of tiny white or pink flowers. She grows intentionally in these pollinator gardens but also shows up uninvited on roadsides, in meadows, and across waste grounds. Yarrow can reach heights of three feet and grow nearly that wide as well, spreading with a rhizomatic root system. Regardless of where she is found, yarrow prefers drought conditions, flowering mid- to late summer (encourage additional blooms by trimming them back as they appear). For the most volatile oils (and her most potent medicine), harvest blooms and leaves three weeks after a drought has passed (clip the entire stem for leaves). As a final identification verification, crush the leaves and inhale. Yarrow smells vaguely of cabbage, chrysanthemums, and, in some cases, licorice. If you smell carrot instead, you have found potentially toxic Queen Anne's lace.

Yarrow is a diaphoretic febrifuge that encourages sweating specifically to break high fevers. She fights infection and is an excellent treatment for colds and flu. Her anti-viral and anti-inflammatory properties are helpful both internally and externally—when applied to bites or stings, she burns but works quickly to heal. Yarrow's best-known use and namesake lies in her hemostatic ability. As a wound wash, yarrow stops bleeding and promotes healthy tissue growth.

A word of caution: yarrow is strong herbal medicine that should only be used for acute illness. She is not to be used as a daily infusion or general support. People who are pregnant should not use yarrow at all, as she can stimulate uterine contractions.

Yarrow's flavor is slightly sweet, like licorice, but finishes bitter and astringent. Because of her taste, her uses tend towards the strictly medicinal.

Suggested preparation

Flu-busting tea: To break fevers and treat colds and flu, combine 1 tablespoon each of yarrow and either elderflower or mint and cover with boiling water. Allow to steep for 15 minutes, then strain and re-heat if needed. Serve with lemon and a dash of honey to boost mood and soothe an irritated throat.

Additionally:

- Tincture leaves and flowers for quick relief of symptoms
- Infuse oil with dried leaves to make a salve or balm
- Create a wash for bites, stings, and wounds

Yarrow (Achillea millefolium)

Millions of tiny white- or
pink- petaled flowers form
clusters on branching stems.

Leaves arrayed in a
spiral pattern
around the
stem.

Largest feathery leaves
at the base of
the plant.

Field Notes

Yellow dock (Rumex crispus)

For plant medicine in all seasons, one with alterative support that boosts the immune system, yellow dock is a good friend. Found under the planet Jupiter, yellow dock has great potential to bring balance to a worn-out or otherwise stressed body. She is particularly associated with the digestive system and with clearing and supporting liver function, but her benefits are wide-ranging throughout the body.

Yellow dock can be found year-round in temperate climates, but new growth typically begins in the spring. Find her everywhere the sun shines upon the earth: vacant lots, roadsides, yards, open fields, the middle of your lawn, the edge of the woods. She thrives in terrible soil and will even grow in piles of garbage when the wind carries her seeds there. First-year yellow dock emerges in a low-growing basal rosette of leaves with ruffled edges (*crispus* is Latin for curly and gives yellow dock another common name—curly dock). These leaves are up to a foot long and narrow - but no more than three inches wide at the base. In her second year, yellow dock begins to flower in June or July. Flowers appear as racemes (separate flowers on short, thin stalks) that swirl up in loosely branched clusters called a panicle. This pattern of flowering is similar to the way in which yellow docks' family of plants (buckwheat) flowers—they appear in groups of ten to 25 small, greenish flowers that are easy to miss. When fall comes, flowers dry up and four-foot tall swords of seed dominate the landscape. Look for loose papery enclosures on a brown stalk all the way through the winter.

Yellow dock's most powerful medicine is in her roots. They have a distinctive yellow color and can grow up to a foot long. Harvest in fall of the first year or spring of the second by inserting a trowel or hori-hori deeply around the base of the plant and easing the roots out while gently tugging upwards on the plant matter.

Yellow dock primarily benefits digestion and liver function. Many believe she is high in iron, but what she actually does is more efficiently free up iron that is stored in the liver. In this way, and in her restoration of proper digestion, yellow dock helps us to make better use of our food and is used to treat cases of malnutrition. She is good for relieving symptoms of IBS, acting as a mild laxative that reduces heat in the digestive tract. Yellow dock's diuretic action treats conditions in the urinary tract (e.g., UTIs and kidney stones). Her anti-inflammatory actions work both inside and out, treating not only arthritis and rheumatism but also inflammatory skin conditions like psoriasis, eczema, and rashes.

A word of caution: the leaves of yellow dock contain oxalic acid. Eaten in large quantities, this can block the body's absorption of calcium and cause a deficiency. Excessive use may also irritate the bowels—proceed slowly.

Yellow dock root is quite bitter, but her young, tender leaves can be harvested just after they open and used as you would spinach (combine with spinach and beets for excellent nutritional support). On the other side of the harvest, yellow dock seeds can be made into flour that is used in the same way as buckwheat flour – think crackers, pancakes, and breads.

Suggested preparation

Yellow dock syrup: This traditional syrup improves nutrient uptake and is great for constipation in people who are pregnant. Chop 2 ounces of yellow dock root and add to a saucepan with 16 ounces of water. Bring to a simmer and keep it there until it reduces by half. Strain into a large measuring cup or pint jar. Note how much liquid you have and add half that amount in blackstrap molasses. Stir until the molasses is melted and cool before bottling.

Additionally:

- Create a wash for inflammatory skin conditions
- Use as a root tincture for digestion and liver support (without added sugar)

Yellow dock * (Rumex crispus)

Ruffle-edged leaves
are up to a foot
long but just
3" wide at
their base

Tall, skinny stems
grow two to
three feet in
the first year.

Roots reach a foot into the
earth and have a distinctive
yellow hue.

*first-year growth

Yellow dock * (Rumex crispus)

Flowers give way to
towering, seed-laden
tapers up to four
feet long.

Imperceptible light
green flowers spiral
around the stem
in loose clusters.

Leaves retain their
characteristic ruffle.

* second-year growth

Field Notes

Afterword

These pandemic years have been hard on city plants.

As more people headed outside to escape the doldrums experienced on their COVID couches, so, too, did the detritus of their lives: food wrappers, cigarette butts, and always the discarded surgical mask that was the must-have accessory of 2020. Wherever we go, there we are, and in 2020 we showed up outside loud, unmannerly, and carrying all sorts of non-biodegradable baggage that we left strewn on the ground.

Yet despite these spikes of human ignorance and apathy, plant life in cities has, paradoxically, largely flourished. Depleted public works departments have prioritized other concerns and left medians and city parks to go to seed. In the wake of this inattention, stands of stinging nettle, yellow dock, and other foragable plants have flourished throughout cities across the country. As the pandemic wore on and people stayed outside, voices became soft and our minds quieted. The anxiety of the year dissolved, even for a moment, in unintended sessions of shinrin—calming forest bathing to reset our taxed parasympathetic nervous system.

For the first half of 2020, traffic noise lessened as people stayed home, and for a brief period of time it became almost possible to experience near-total quiet in pocket parks and along forested trails through cities.

We are now many of us returning to jobs and lives outside of our pandemic bunkers. Leaf blowers and lawn mowers are once again ringing out, and downtown corridors are packed with cars and their noise.

In Maryland, the Brood X cicadas emerged mid-May 2021 after a 17-year slumber, crawling out of pencil-thin holes in the dark to scale the trees that nourished them as they slept. And then for weeks, as the sun reached its mid-morning height, the males expanded the tymbals underneath their wings to create their signature summer buzz. The females responded with clicks. The noise was overwhelming and full-body.

Visceral.

In this way, the cicadas called to us, cacophonously, to not forget what we have learned in our time outside in 2020. To stay rooted to the ground where we are growing and to lift our eyes up to the swaying tops of trees to experience the immensity of our universe and our place within it.

Even as we move back into the rhythm of civilization, it is my hope that something of the wildness of this pandemic year will remain with us—the smell of rain on a dusty path, the thin winter sun on our faces, the sounds of creatures in city parks.

Let this wildness be in us as we are in it. Happy foraging.

Suzannah
June 2021

Additional Resources

Diaz, J. (2020). *Plant Witchery: Discover the Sacred Language, Wisdom, and Magic of 200 Plants*. Hay House, Inc. Juliet Diaz brings together magical wisdom and herbal lore for 200 plants in this easy-to-use introduction to plant witchery.

Easley, T., & Horne, S. H. (2016). *The Modern Herbal Dispensatory: A Medicine-Making Guide*. North Atlantic Books. When you are serious about building an herbal apothecary and need a detailed instruction manual, turn to this book of 250 herbal medicines for over 100 different ailments. More advanced preparations are covered here, too.

Gladstar, R. (2012). *Rosemary Gladstar's Medicinal Herbs: A Beginner's Guide: 33 Healing Herbs to Know, Grow, and Use*. Storey Books. Rosemary Gladstar is a widely respected herbalist who has been making (and teaching about) herbal medicine for nearly half a century. This book includes 124 recipes that utilize 33 plants in a variety of preparations.

Kimmerer, R. W. (2013). *Braiding Sweetgrass*. Milkweed Editions. As an enrolled member of the Citizen Potawatomi Nation, Robin Wall Kimmerer looks at the plant world through eyes that are educated through generational wisdom and respect. As a scientist, she marries scientific research with practical application. I highly recommend this book for anyone beginning (or renewing) their relationship with nature.

Meyer, J. E., & Meyer, J. E. (1979). *The herbalist: Medicinal plants, Plant Vitamins & Minerals, Beverage Teas, Spices & Flavoring Herbs, Plant Colors for Food & Cosmetics, Plant Dyes for Fabrics, Botanicals for Potpourri & Sachets, Dentifrices, Gargles, Cosmetics, Botanicalcurios, Smoke Flavoring Botanicals, Assorted Other Information*. Meyerbooks. This handy (if old-fashioned) book provides simple descriptions of plants that include their medicinal parts, a brief description, their properties, and dosing suggestions. It also includes recipe suggestions and instructions for preparations (including how to extract the odor of flowers).

Mills, S., & Bone, K. (2005). *The Essential Guide to Herbal Safety*. Elsevier Churchill Livingstone. Because of the personalized nature of herbal remedies, a safety guide is important. This book helps uncover potential interactions, allergies, levels of toxicity, and counter-indications for 125 herbs.

Potterton, D. (1997). *Culpeper's Colour Herbal*. Foulsham. From the father of an astrological interpretation of plants and their actions comes this illustrated herbal that features 16th century's Nicholas Culpeper's pointed advice on plants and their uses. Working with impoverished patients in London, Culpeper was enraged by apothecaries of the time that exploited poor patients' ignorance of medicine and often sold them expensive, useless potions. He prescribed instead "the peoples' medicine" of plant remedies, encouraging patients to seek out healing plants on their own.

Wood, M., & Ryan, D. (2016). *The Earthwise Herbal Repertory: The Definitive Practitioner's Guide*. North Atlantic Books. Another excellent resource that not only looks at a plant's basic actions and properties but also considers the energetics and systems that are affected by each. It is a more holistic way to look at working with herbal remedies than simply identifying the condition and a plant's effects on it.

YouTube. (n.d.). *Black Forager* (Alexis Smith). YouTube. Retrieved March 28, 2022, from youtube.com/c/BlackForager Alexis Nelson is an enthusiatic, highly knowledgeable forager based in Columbus, Ohio. She offers brief tidbits of foraging wisdom and recipes on the cited YouTube channel, Instagram (@(blackforager), and TikTok (Alexisnikole).

YouTube. (n.d.). *She is of the Woods*. YouTube. Retrieved March 28, 2022, from youtube.com/c/ColdCreekHomestead/videos April Graham runs an herbal apothecary on her homestead. Her stated mission is to convince everyone that they are smart enough to treat themselves with herbal remedies, and her YouTube channel is packed with long instructional videos and details about the medicinal properties and uses of the plants she forages to make medicine. In the future, April plans to open her homestead to a limited number of herbal interns who will help with the work of the homestead while learning about foraging and medicine-making.

Bios

Suzannah Kolbeck writes and paints in Baltimore, Maryland. She is the co-author of *The Food Market at Home*, and her work has appeared in *Plainsongs*, *Pomme Journal*, *50Haikus*, and *The Chicago Tribune*.

Transplanted from the south, **Kim Mattison** blooms in Baltimore. This book's lines and scribbles are dedicated to her plant-loving mama, gramma, and husband.

www.ingramcontent.com/pod-product-compliance
Lightning Source LLC
Chambersburg PA
CBHW052024030426
42335CB00026B/3268